Published by Little King Publishing 2019

Copyright © Tommy Gray 2019

All rights reserved. This book or any portion thereof may not be reproduced or used in any manner whatsoever without the express written permission of the publisher except for the use of brief quotations in a book review.

ISBN 978-1-5272-1935-9

Little King Publishing
39 Leinster Park, Harold's Cross,
Dublin 6W

theideasjournal.com

Available to retailers worldwide from INGRAM Book Company.

The Ideas Journal is manufactured on-demand meaning units are only produced as they are ordered reducing excess production and waste.

The purpose of print-on-demand book manufacturing is to reduce our environmental impact by minimising supply chain waste, greenhouse emissions, and conserving valuable natural resources.

Paper is provided by environmentally responsible suppliers who do not use papers sourced from endangered old-growth forests, forests of exceptional conservation value, or the Amazon Basin.

dedicated

To those who have had big ideas and made them happen.

ideation
noun

The formation of ideas or concepts.

problem solution ideation
noun

Finding a problem and solving it.

derivative ideation
noun

Taking something that already exists and changing it.

symbiotic ideation
noun

Combining multiple existing ideas to create one new idea.

revolutionary ideation
noun

Breaking away from conventional thought and creating a brand new perspective.

introduction

Hello and welcome to *The Ideas Journal*. This is a place to create new ideas for the things you are passionate about. A place to create new possibilities for the future. A place to get inspired and imagine more.

To create truly great ideas you must become an "ideas person". What does that mean? When others see nothing special, you see potential. When others see just one option, you see ten. When others see a life laid out for them with only one narrow path, you see an open plain waiting for you to build your own world.

Becoming an ideas person means becoming deeply interested in life and the people around you, understanding what drives us, and having a genuine desire to make things better. The greatest ideas people have always been this way. Steve Jobs, for example, wasn't really interested in phones and computers. He was interested in people and how they interact with technology, and he was passionate about evolving that relationship to improve our lives.

If you fill your life with passion and curiosity, and make a habit of creating ideas which make things better, you will have light-bulb moments that light up the whole world. That's what *The Ideas Journal* is all about.

HOW CAN I MAKE THINGS BETTER?

From this one question an infinity of answers will come. Ask it often. Make it a habit. It will always have an answer, and it will always lead to positive action. It can be asked of your health, your finances, your relationships, your career, technology, politics, the environment. If this question was asked by everyone everyday, and if everyone produced answers to this question and took action to make those ideas happen, the world would be a better place. *The Ideas Journal* provides a place to write 100 answers to this important question.

MAKE YOUR IDEAS HAPPEN

Showing people your ideas is always better than telling people your ideas. Whether you are an entrepreneur compiling business start-up ideas or an artist compiling project ideas, remember that coming up with a good idea is just the beginning. Ideas require action. Writing a shopping list will not put food in your belly. *The Ideas Journal* is designed with action in mind.

> " The critical ingredient is getting off your butt and doing something. It's as simple as that. A lot of people have ideas, but there are few who decide to do something about them now. Not tomorrow, not next week, but today. The true entrepreneur is a doer, not a dreamer. "
>
> —**NOLAN BUSHNELL**
> **Co-founder of Atari**

instructions

THE TITLE

Giving something a name snaps it out of abstraction and into the real world. Take the time to think of a title which makes you excited about your idea. Maybe the Title will be the first section you complete—many songs have begun with just the song title, and the rest came from there—or maybe it will be the last section you fill in, and after spending time on all the other details perhaps the title may be calling out to you.

THE TAGLINE

Can you describe your idea in one sentence? Often this is harder than it sounds. But it can be crucial if you meet a potential investor in an elevator, or if you need a snappy heading for your product advertising. It can be important, too, just for ourselves to crystallise our concept, making it clear and unified. Rumour has it that Arnold Schwarzenegger when asked to read a movie script would say, "Show me the poster." If the producer couldn't convey their idea with only an image, title, and tagline, Arnold didn't want to waste his time reading the whole script.

STEP ONE

Every idea has a point of entry, the first step which will make all additional steps possible. When Richard Branson had an idea to start an airline company, his Step One was to call Boeing and ask the cost of leasing a second-hand 747. You can't start an airline company without a plane! But many of us might have spent days doodling with logo ideas, or thinking of what colour the flight crew's uniforms should be. Step One is about executing on your idea and taking a real step towards making it happen.

ADDITIONAL STEPS

Think through the process very carefully. Think of everything which needs to be done. Use the Notes page to write down all the steps you can think of in no particular order, then look through everything and form a clear road map from start to finish. Finally, write down the key steps in order. Every idea will have its own number of steps. Write down as many as possible. Make each step a clear action which you know how to begin and you will know when you have completed. Never add filler in this section just because you feel you ought to write something there. You don't want to end up busying yourself with tasks which make you feel like you're doing something, when in fact you are no closer to your goal. If all you've got is Step One, execute that to the letter. The next step will become obvious once you have taken some action.

WHY

In this section you might write, "I'll be rich!" Or maybe you'll write, "This idea will help thousands of people." You can measure the worth of your ideas by what you write in the Why section. Make your *why*s big and you are guaranteed to have big ideas.

GENIUS RATING

Tackle this only once the rest is complete. Never judge your idea while it is forming. Train yourself to separate judgement from creativity and your creativity will flourish. Treat each idea as though it were your best yet. Then once you have gotten it all written down, give it some real, objective thought and circle a number indicating whether it is:

1. A good idea
2. An amazing idea
3. Pure genius

IDEAS INDEX

When you have completed a new idea entry, add the Title and Genius Rating beside the relevant Idea N° in the Ideas Index. This will serve as your table of contents. Each of the 100 templates has a corresponding Idea N° in the top right corner.

" Nothing is impossible. The word itself says, "I'm possible." "

—**AUDREY HEPBURN**
Actress, *Breakfast at Tiffany's*

IDEAS INDEX

IDEA N°	TITLE	GENIUS RATING
1.		1 2 3
2.		1 2 3
3.		1 2 3
4.		1 2 3
5.		1 2 3
6.		1 2 3
7.		1 2 3
8.		1 2 3
9.		1 2 3
10.		1 2 3
11.		1 2 3
12.		1 2 3
13.		1 2 3
14.		1 2 3
15.		1 2 3
16.		1 2 3
17.		1 2 3
18.		1 2 3
19.		1 2 3
20.		1 2 3
21.		1 2 3
22.		1 2 3
23.		1 2 3
24.		1 2 3
25.		1 2 3

IDEAS INDEX

IDEA Nº	TITLE	GENIUS RATING
26.		1 2 3
27.		1 2 3
28.		1 2 3
29.		1 2 3
30.		1 2 3
31.		1 2 3
32.		1 2 3
33.		1 2 3
34.		1 2 3
35.		1 2 3
36.		1 2 3
37.		1 2 3
38.		1 2 3
39.		1 2 3
40.		1 2 3
41.		1 2 3
42.		1 2 3
43.		1 2 3
44.		1 2 3
45.		1 2 3
46.		1 2 3
47.		1 2 3
48.		1 2 3
49.		1 2 3
50.		1 2 3

IDEAS INDEX

IDEA N°	TITLE	GENIUS RATING
51.		1 2 3
52.		1 2 3
53.		1 2 3
54.		1 2 3
55.		1 2 3
56.		1 2 3
57.		1 2 3
58.		1 2 3
59.		1 2 3
60.		1 2 3
61.		1 2 3
62.		1 2 3
63.		1 2 3
64.		1 2 3
65.		1 2 3
66.		1 2 3
67.		1 2 3
68.		1 2 3
69.		1 2 3
70.		1 2 3
71.		1 2 3
72.		1 2 3
73.		1 2 3
74.		1 2 3
75.		1 2 3

IDEAS INDEX

IDEA N°	TITLE	GENIUS RATING		
76.		1	2	3
77.		1	2	3
78.		1	2	3
79.		1	2	3
80.		1	2	3
81.		1	2	3
82.		1	2	3
83.		1	2	3
84.		1	2	3
85.		1	2	3
86.		1	2	3
87.		1	2	3
88.		1	2	3
89.		1	2	3
90.		1	2	3
91.		1	2	3
92.		1	2	3
93.		1	2	3
94.		1	2	3
95.		1	2	3
96.		1	2	3
97.		1	2	3
98.		1	2	3
99.		1	2	3
100.		1	2	3

___/___/___

TITLE: _____
(GIVE IT A NAME)

TAG: _____
(DEFINE IT)

STEP ONE
(MAKE THIS SOMETHING YOU CAN DO RIGHT NOW)

_____ ☐

ADDITIONAL STEPS
(THE PLAN)

_____ ☐
_____ ☐
_____ ☐
_____ ☐
_____ ☐

WHY?:
(GIVE IT A PURPOSE)

_____
_____

GENIUS RATING

1   **2**   **3**

NOTES   **IDEA Nº 1**

> If you've got an idea that you genuinely think is good, don't let some idiot talk you out of it.
>
> —**STAN LEE**
> **Comic book writer at Marvel Comics**
> **Creator of Spider-Man**

___ / ___ / ___

TITLE: _____
(GIVE IT A NAME)

TAG: _____
(DEFINE IT)

STEP ONE
(MAKE THIS SOMETHING YOU CAN DO RIGHT NOW)

_____ ☐

ADDITIONAL STEPS
(THE PLAN)

_____ ☐
_____ ☐
_____ ☐
_____ ☐
_____ ☐

WHY?:
(GIVE IT A PURPOSE)

_____
_____

GENIUS RATING

1   2   3

NOTES   **IDEA N⁰ 2**

> New ideas pass through three periods:
> 1. It can't be done.
> 2. It probably can be done, but it's not worth doing.
> 3. I knew it was a good idea all along!

—ARTHUR C. CLARKE
Author of *2001: A Space Odyssey*

___/___/___

TITLE: _____
(GIVE IT A NAME)

TAG: _____
(DEFINE IT)

STEP ONE
(MAKE THIS SOMETHING YOU CAN DO RIGHT NOW)

_____ ☐

ADDITIONAL STEPS
(THE PLAN)

_____ ☐
_____ ☐
_____ ☐
_____ ☐
_____ ☐

WHY?:
(GIVE IT A PURPOSE)

_____
_____

GENIUS RATING

1   2   3

NOTES **IDEA Nº 3**

> " In whatever you do, you're not going to stand out unless you think big and have ideas that are truly original. That comes from tapping into your own creativity, not obsessing over what everyone else is doing. "
>
> —**SOPHIA AMORUSO**
> **Author of *#GIRLBOSS***

____/____/____

TITLE: _____
(GIVE IT A NAME)

TAG: _____
(DEFINE IT)

STEP ONE
(MAKE THIS SOMETHING YOU CAN DO RIGHT NOW)

_____ ☐

ADDITIONAL STEPS
(THE PLAN)

_____ ☐
_____ ☐
_____ ☐
_____ ☐
_____ ☐

WHY?:
(GIVE IT A PURPOSE)

_____
_____

GENIUS RATING

1   **2**   **3**

NOTES   **IDEA N° 4**

> When you write down your ideas you automatically focus your full attention on them. Few if any of us can write one thought and think another at the same time. Thus a pencil and paper make excellent concentration tools.

—**MICHAEL LEBOEUF**
Author of *The Greatest Management Principle in the World*

___ / ___ / _____

TITLE: _____
(GIVE IT A NAME)

TAG: _____
(DEFINE IT)

STEP ONE
(MAKE THIS SOMETHING YOU CAN DO RIGHT NOW)

_____ ☐

ADDITIONAL STEPS
(THE PLAN)

_____ ☐
_____ ☐
_____ ☐
_____ ☐
_____ ☐

WHY?:
(GIVE IT A PURPOSE)

_____
_____

GENIUS RATING

1   2   3

NOTES **IDEA N⁰ 5**

> People say ideas are a dime a dozen. That's kinda B.S. It's hard to come up with a good idea. If you write down ten ideas a day—that's 3,650 ideas a year—one of them might be a good idea.
>
> **—JAMES ALTUCHER**
> **Author of *The Choose Yourself Guide to Wealth***

___/___/___

TITLE: _____
(GIVE IT A NAME)

TAG: _____
(DEFINE IT)

STEP ONE
(MAKE THIS SOMETHING YOU CAN DO RIGHT NOW)

_____ ☐

ADDITIONAL STEPS
(THE PLAN)

_____ ☐
_____ ☐
_____ ☐
_____ ☐
_____ ☐

WHY?:
(GIVE IT A PURPOSE)

_____
_____

GENIUS RATING

1   **2**   **3**

NOTES   **IDEA Nº 6**

> Ideas are like rabbits. You get a couple and learn how to handle them, and pretty soon you have a dozen.
>
> —JOHN STEINBECK
> **Author of *The Grapes of Wrath***

___ / ___ / ___

TITLE: _____
(GIVE IT A NAME)

TAG: _____
(DEFINE IT)

STEP ONE
(MAKE THIS SOMETHING YOU CAN DO RIGHT NOW)

_____ ☐

ADDITIONAL STEPS
(THE PLAN)

_____ ☐
_____ ☐
_____ ☐
_____ ☐
_____ ☐

WHY?:
(GIVE IT A PURPOSE)

_____
_____

GENIUS RATING

1   **2**   **3**

NOTES   **IDEA Nº 7**

> "Take the first step in faith. You don't have to see the whole staircase, just take the first step."
>
> —**DR. MARTIN LUTHER KING JR.**
> **Leader in the American Civil Rights Movement**

___/___/___

TITLE: _____
(GIVE IT A NAME)

TAG: _____
(DEFINE IT)

STEP ONE
(MAKE THIS SOMETHING YOU CAN DO RIGHT NOW)

_____ ☐

ADDITIONAL STEPS
(THE PLAN)

_____ ☐
_____ ☐
_____ ☐
_____ ☐
_____ ☐

WHY?:
(GIVE IT A PURPOSE)

_____
_____

GENIUS RATING

1 **2** **3**

NOTES   **IDEA N° 8**

> Ideas are worthless without execution, and execution is pointless without ideas.
>
> —**GARY VAYNERCHUK**
> **Co-founder and CEO of VaynerMedia**

_____ / _____ / _____

TITLE: _____
(GIVE IT A NAME)

TAG: _____
(DEFINE IT)

STEP ONE
(MAKE THIS SOMETHING YOU CAN DO RIGHT NOW)

_____ ☐

ADDITIONAL STEPS
(THE PLAN)

_____ ☐
_____ ☐
_____ ☐
_____ ☐
_____ ☐

WHY?:
(GIVE IT A PURPOSE)

_____
_____

GENIUS RATING

1   2   3

NOTES   **IDEA Nº 9**

> "I've had periods in my life when I've had a bundle of ideas come along, and I've had long dry spells. If I get an idea next week, I'll do something. If not, I won't do a damn thing."
>
> —**WARREN BUFFET**
> **Investor**
> **CEO of Berkshire Hathaway**

___ / ___ / _____

TITLE: _____
(GIVE IT A NAME)

TAG: _____
(DEFINE IT)

STEP ONE
(MAKE THIS SOMETHING YOU CAN DO RIGHT NOW)

_____ ☐

ADDITIONAL STEPS
(THE PLAN)

_____ ☐
_____ ☐
_____ ☐
_____ ☐
_____ ☐

WHY?:
(GIVE IT A PURPOSE)

_____
_____

GENIUS RATING

1   2   3

NOTES　　　　　　　　　　　　　　　　　　　**IDEA Nº 10**

> " The way to get started is to quit talking and begin doing. "
>
> **—WALT DISNEY**
> **Co-founder of the Walt Disney Company**

___ / ___ / ___

TITLE: _____
(GIVE IT A NAME)

TAG: _____
(DEFINE IT)

STEP ONE
(MAKE THIS SOMETHING YOU CAN DO RIGHT NOW)

_____ ☐

ADDITIONAL STEPS
(THE PLAN)

_____ ☐
_____ ☐
_____ ☐
_____ ☐
_____ ☐

WHY?:
(GIVE IT A PURPOSE)

_____
_____

GENIUS RATING

1   **2**   **3**

NOTES   **IDEA N° 11**

> If it's a good idea, go ahead and do it. It's easier to ask forgiveness than it is to get permission.
>
> —**DR. GRACE MURRAY HOPPER**
> **Computer Scientist**
> "Mother of COBOL computer language"

___ / ___ / ___

TITLE: _____
(GIVE IT A NAME)

TAG: _____
(DEFINE IT)

STEP ONE
(MAKE THIS SOMETHING YOU CAN DO RIGHT NOW)

_____ ☐

ADDITIONAL STEPS
(THE PLAN)

_____ ☐
_____ ☐
_____ ☐
_____ ☐
_____ ☐

WHY?:
(GIVE IT A PURPOSE)

_____
_____

GENIUS RATING

1   2   3

NOTES **IDEA Nº 12**

> "The way to get good ideas is to get lots of ideas and throw the bad ones away."
>
> —DR. LINUS PAULING
> **Chemist and peace activist**
> **Nobel Prize in Chemistry and Nobel Peace Prize**

___/___/___

TITLE: _____
(GIVE IT A NAME)

TAG: _____
(DEFINE IT)

STEP ONE
(MAKE THIS SOMETHING YOU CAN DO RIGHT NOW)

_____ ☐

ADDITIONAL STEPS
(THE PLAN)

_____ ☐
_____ ☐
_____ ☐
_____ ☐
_____ ☐

WHY?:
(GIVE IT A PURPOSE)

_____
_____

GENIUS RATING

1   **2**   **3**

NOTES   **IDEA Nº 13**

> What do I think will help a lot of people, and most certainly will help me?

—**MARION DONOVAN**
Inventor of the first waterproof disposable diaper

_____ / _____ / _____

TITLE: _____
(GIVE IT A NAME)

TAG: _____
(DEFINE IT)

STEP ONE
(MAKE THIS SOMETHING YOU CAN DO RIGHT NOW)

_____ ☐

ADDITIONAL STEPS
(THE PLAN)

_____ ☐
_____ ☐
_____ ☐
_____ ☐
_____ ☐

WHY?:
(GIVE IT A PURPOSE)

_____
_____

GENIUS RATING

   1   **2**   **3**

NOTES **IDEA Nº 14**

> If you've got an idea, start today. There's no better time than now to get going. That doesn't mean quit your job and jump into your idea 100 percent from day one, but there's always small progress that can be made to start the movement.
>
> —**KEVIN SYSTROM**
> **Co-founder and CEO of Instagram**

____/____/____

TITLE: _____
(GIVE IT A NAME)

TAG: _____
(DEFINE IT)

STEP ONE
(MAKE THIS SOMETHING YOU CAN DO RIGHT NOW)

_____ ☐

ADDITIONAL STEPS
(THE PLAN)

_____ ☐
_____ ☐
_____ ☐
_____ ☐
_____ ☐

WHY?:
(GIVE IT A PURPOSE)

_____
_____

GENIUS RATING

1   2   3

NOTES **IDEA Nº 15**

> Don't ask yourself, 'How could I design a smartphone?' Ask yourself, 'What is communication?' If you start there, you may be able to discover new possibilities.

—SOOSHIN CHOI
CEO & CDO at The Modus Design

___/___/___

TITLE: _____
(GIVE IT A NAME)

TAG: _____
(DEFINE IT)

STEP ONE
(MAKE THIS SOMETHING YOU CAN DO RIGHT NOW)

_____ ☐

ADDITIONAL STEPS
(THE PLAN)

_____ ☐
_____ ☐
_____ ☐
_____ ☐
_____ ☐

WHY?:
(GIVE IT A PURPOSE)

_____
_____

GENIUS RATING

1   2   3

NOTES   **IDEA Nº 16**

> "If you spot an opportunity and are really excited by it, throw yourself into it with everything you've got."
>
> **—RICHARD BRANSON**
> **Founder of the Virgin Group**

___ / ___ / ___

TITLE: _____
(GIVE IT A NAME)

TAG: _____
(DEFINE IT)

STEP ONE
(MAKE THIS SOMETHING YOU CAN DO RIGHT NOW)

_____ ☐

ADDITIONAL STEPS
(THE PLAN)

_____ ☐
_____ ☐
_____ ☐
_____ ☐
_____ ☐

WHY?:
(GIVE IT A PURPOSE)

_____
_____

GENIUS RATING

1   2   3

NOTES **IDEA N° 17**

> " Night time is really the best time to work. All the ideas are there to be yours because everyone else is asleep. "
>
> —CATHERINE O'HARA
> Actress, *Home Alone*

_____ / _____ / _____

TITLE: _____
(GIVE IT A NAME)

TAG: _____
(DEFINE IT)

STEP ONE
(MAKE THIS SOMETHING YOU CAN DO RIGHT NOW)

_____ ☐

ADDITIONAL STEPS
(THE PLAN)

_____ ☐
_____ ☐
_____ ☐
_____ ☐
_____ ☐

WHY?:
(GIVE IT A PURPOSE)

_____
_____

GENIUS RATING

1   **2**   **3**

NOTES   **IDEA Nº 18**

> " Success is never accidental. "
>
> —**JACK DORSEY**
> **Co-founder and CEO of Twitter**

___ / ___ / ___

TITLE: _____
(GIVE IT A NAME)

TAG: _____
(DEFINE IT)

STEP ONE
(MAKE THIS SOMETHING YOU CAN DO RIGHT NOW)

_____ ☐

ADDITIONAL STEPS
(THE PLAN)

_____ ☐
_____ ☐
_____ ☐
_____ ☐
_____ ☐

WHY?:
(GIVE IT A PURPOSE)

_____
_____

GENIUS RATING

1   2   3

NOTES **IDEA N° 19**

> " Twenty years from now you will be more disappointed by the things that you didn't do than by the ones you did do. "
>
> —MARK TWAIN
> **Author of *Adventures of Huckleberry Finn***

____/____/____

TITLE: _____
(GIVE IT A NAME)

TAG: _____
(DEFINE IT)

STEP ONE
(MAKE THIS SOMETHING YOU CAN DO RIGHT NOW)

_____ ☐

ADDITIONAL STEPS
(THE PLAN)

_____ ☐
_____ ☐
_____ ☐
_____ ☐
_____ ☐

WHY?:
(GIVE IT A PURPOSE)

_____
_____

GENIUS RATING

1   2   3

NOTES   **IDEA N° 20**

> People who succeed at the highest level are not lucky; they're doing something differently than everyone else.
>
> —**TONY ROBBINS**
> **Motivational Speaker**
> **Author of *Awaken the Giant Within***

___/___/___

TITLE: _____
(GIVE IT A NAME)

TAG: _____
(DEFINE IT)

STEP ONE
(MAKE THIS SOMETHING YOU CAN DO RIGHT NOW)

☐
_____

ADDITIONAL STEPS
(THE PLAN)

_____ ☐
_____ ☐
_____ ☐
_____ ☐
_____ ☐

WHY?:
(GIVE IT A PURPOSE)

_____
_____

GENIUS RATING

1   **2**   **3**

NOTES **IDEA Nº 21**

" You need a stubborn belief in an idea in order to see it realised. "

—JAMES DYSON
Industrial Designer
Founder of Dyson Ltd

___/___/___

TITLE: _____
(GIVE IT A NAME)

TAG: _____
(DEFINE IT)

STEP ONE
(MAKE THIS SOMETHING YOU CAN DO RIGHT NOW)

_____ ☐

ADDITIONAL STEPS
(THE PLAN)

_____ ☐
_____ ☐
_____ ☐
_____ ☐
_____ ☐

WHY?:
(GIVE IT A PURPOSE)

_____
_____

GENIUS RATING

1   2   3

NOTES   **IDEA Nº 22**

> "An entrepreneur is someone who jumps off a cliff and builds a plane on the way down."
>
> —**REID HOFFMAN**
> **Co-founder of LinkedIn**

____/____/____

TITLE: _____
(GIVE IT A NAME)

TAG: _____
(DEFINE IT)

STEP ONE
(MAKE THIS SOMETHING YOU CAN DO RIGHT NOW)

_____ ☐

ADDITIONAL STEPS
(THE PLAN)

_____ ☐
_____ ☐
_____ ☐
_____ ☐
_____ ☐

WHY?:
(GIVE IT A PURPOSE)

_____
_____

GENIUS RATING

1   2   3

NOTES   **IDEA N° 23**

> For all of the most important things, the timing always sucks. Waiting for a good time to quit your job? The stars will never align and the traffic lights of life will never all be green at the same time. The universe doesn't conspire against you, but it doesn't go out of its way to line up the pins either. Conditions are never perfect.

—**TIM FERRISS**
Author of *The 4-Hour Work Week*

___ / ___ / ___

TITLE: _____
(GIVE IT A NAME)

TAG: _____
(DEFINE IT)

STEP ONE
(MAKE THIS SOMETHING YOU CAN DO RIGHT NOW)

☐

ADDITIONAL STEPS
(THE PLAN)

☐
☐
☐
☐
☐

WHY?:
(GIVE IT A PURPOSE)

GENIUS RATING

1   **2**   **3**

NOTES **IDEA Nº 24**

" Plan your work for today and every day, then work your plan. "

—**MARGARET THATCHER**
Former British Prime Minister

___/___/___

TITLE: _____
(GIVE IT A NAME)

TAG: _____
(DEFINE IT)

STEP ONE
(MAKE THIS SOMETHING YOU CAN DO RIGHT NOW)

_____ ☐

ADDITIONAL STEPS
(THE PLAN)

_____ ☐
_____ ☐
_____ ☐
_____ ☐
_____ ☐

WHY?:
(GIVE IT A PURPOSE)

_____
_____

GENIUS RATING

1   **2**   **3**

NOTES   **IDEA N° 25**

> Capital isn't that important in business. Experience isn't that important. You can get both of these things. What is important is ideas.

—**HARVEY S. FIRESTONE**
Founder of Firestone Tire and Rubber Company

_____ / _____ / _____

TITLE: _____
(GIVE IT A NAME)

TAG: _____
(DEFINE IT)

STEP ONE
(MAKE THIS SOMETHING YOU CAN DO RIGHT NOW)

_____ ☐

ADDITIONAL STEPS
(THE PLAN)

_____ ☐
_____ ☐
_____ ☐
_____ ☐
_____ ☐

WHY?:
(GIVE IT A PURPOSE)

_____
_____

GENIUS RATING

1   **2**   **3**

NOTES   **IDEA N° 26**

> If you hear a voice within you say, 'You cannot paint,' then by all means paint, and that voice will be silenced.

—**VINCENT VAN GOGH**
Painter, *The Starry Night*

___ / ___ / _____

TITLE: _____
(GIVE IT A NAME)

TAG: _____
(DEFINE IT)

STEP ONE
(MAKE THIS SOMETHING YOU CAN DO RIGHT NOW)

_____ ☐

ADDITIONAL STEPS
(THE PLAN)

_____ ☐
_____ ☐
_____ ☐
_____ ☐
_____ ☐

WHY?:
(GIVE IT A PURPOSE)

_____
_____

GENIUS RATING

1   **2**   **3**

NOTES   **IDEA N° 27**

> Often the difference between a successful person and a failure is not one's better abilities or ideas, but the courage that one has to bet on their idea, to take a calculated risk, and to act.
>
> —**MAXWELL MALTZ**
> **Cosmetic Surgeon**
> **Author of *Psycho-Cybernetics***

___/___/___

TITLE: _____
(GIVE IT A NAME)

TAG: _____
(DEFINE IT)

STEP ONE
(MAKE THIS SOMETHING YOU CAN DO RIGHT NOW)

_____ ☐

ADDITIONAL STEPS
(THE PLAN)

_____ ☐
_____ ☐
_____ ☐
_____ ☐
_____ ☐

WHY?:
(GIVE IT A PURPOSE)

_____
_____

GENIUS RATING

1   **2**   **3**

NOTES **IDEA Nº 28**

> "Your time is limited, so don't waste it living someone else's life."
>
> —STEVE JOBS
> **Co-founder and CEO of Apple**

___/___/___

TITLE: _____
(GIVE IT A NAME)

TAG: _____
(DEFINE IT)

STEP ONE
(MAKE THIS SOMETHING YOU CAN DO RIGHT NOW)

_____ ☐

ADDITIONAL STEPS
(THE PLAN)

_____ ☐
_____ ☐
_____ ☐
_____ ☐
_____ ☐

WHY?:
(GIVE IT A PURPOSE)

_____
_____

GENIUS RATING

1 2 3

NOTES   **IDEA N° 29**

> When I am completely myself, entirely alone, or during the night when I cannot sleep, it is on such occasions that my ideas flow best and most abundantly. Whence and how these ideas come I know not, nor can I force them.
>
> —**WOLFGANG AMADEUS MOZART**
> **Composer,** *The Marriage of Figaro*

___ / ___ / ___

TITLE: _____
(GIVE IT A NAME)

TAG: _____
(DEFINE IT)

STEP ONE
(MAKE THIS SOMETHING YOU CAN DO RIGHT NOW)

_____ ☐

ADDITIONAL STEPS
(THE PLAN)

_____ ☐
_____ ☐
_____ ☐
_____ ☐
_____ ☐

WHY?:
(GIVE IT A PURPOSE)

_____
_____

GENIUS RATING

1   2   3

NOTES   **IDEA Nº 30**

> "I learned to always take on things I'd never done before. Growth and comfort do not coexist."
>
> **—GINNI ROMETTY**
> **Chairman, President, and CEO of IBM**

___ / ___ / ___

TITLE: _____
(GIVE IT A NAME)

TAG: _____
(DEFINE IT)

STEP ONE
(MAKE THIS SOMETHING YOU CAN DO RIGHT NOW)

_____ ☐

ADDITIONAL STEPS
(THE PLAN)

_____ ☐
_____ ☐
_____ ☐
_____ ☐
_____ ☐

WHY?:
(GIVE IT A PURPOSE)

_____
_____

GENIUS RATING

1   2   3

NOTES   **IDEA N° 31**

> Always carry a notebook. And I mean always. The short-term memory only retains information for three minutes; unless it is committed to paper you can lose an idea for ever.

—**WILL SELF**
Author of *Umbrella*

_____ / _____ / _____

TITLE: _____
(GIVE IT A NAME)

TAG: _____
(DEFINE IT)

STEP ONE
(MAKE THIS SOMETHING YOU CAN DO RIGHT NOW)

_____ ☐

ADDITIONAL STEPS
(THE PLAN)

_____ ☐
_____ ☐
_____ ☐
_____ ☐
_____ ☐

WHY?:
(GIVE IT A PURPOSE)

_____
_____

GENIUS RATING

1   2   3

NOTES   **IDEA Nº 32**

> "If you have a good idea, use it so that you will not only accomplish something, but so that you can make room for new ones to flow into you."
>
> —MING-DAO DENG
> Author of *365 Tao: Daily Meditations*

_____ / _____ / _____

TITLE: _____
(GIVE IT A NAME)

TAG: _____
(DEFINE IT)

STEP ONE
(MAKE THIS SOMETHING YOU CAN DO RIGHT NOW)

_____ ☐

ADDITIONAL STEPS
(THE PLAN)

_____ ☐
_____ ☐
_____ ☐
_____ ☐
_____ ☐

WHY?:
(GIVE IT A PURPOSE)

_____
_____

GENIUS RATING

1   **2**   **3**

NOTES **IDEA Nº 33**

> A good idea always attracts other good ideas.
>
> —**PATRICK NESS**
> **Author of *A Monster Calls***

___/___/___

TITLE: _____
(GIVE IT A NAME)

TAG: _____
(DEFINE IT)

STEP ONE
(MAKE THIS SOMETHING YOU CAN DO RIGHT NOW)

_____ ☐

ADDITIONAL STEPS
(THE PLAN)

_____ ☐
_____ ☐
_____ ☐
_____ ☐
_____ ☐

WHY?:
(GIVE IT A PURPOSE)

_____
_____

GENIUS RATING

1   2   3

NOTES **IDEA N° 34**

> " Surround yourself with people who believe in your dreams, encourage your ideas, support your ambitions, and bring out the best in you. "

—ROY BENNETT
Member of the Senate of Zimbabwe

___/___/___

TITLE: _____
(GIVE IT A NAME)

TAG: _____
(DEFINE IT)

STEP ONE
(MAKE THIS SOMETHING YOU CAN DO RIGHT NOW)

_____ ☐

ADDITIONAL STEPS
(THE PLAN)

_____ ☐
_____ ☐
_____ ☐
_____ ☐
_____ ☐

WHY?:
(GIVE IT A PURPOSE)

_____
_____

GENIUS RATING

1   2   3

NOTES **IDEA Nº 35**

> Rules are a great way to get ideas. All you have to do is break them.
>
> —**JACK FOSTER**
> Author of *How to Get Ideas*

___/___/___

TITLE: _____
(GIVE IT A NAME)

TAG: _____
(DEFINE IT)

STEP ONE
(MAKE THIS SOMETHING YOU CAN DO RIGHT NOW)

_____ ☐

ADDITIONAL STEPS
(THE PLAN)

_____ ☐
_____ ☐
_____ ☐
_____ ☐
_____ ☐

WHY?:
(GIVE IT A PURPOSE)

_____
_____

GENIUS RATING

1   **2**   **3**

NOTES   **IDEA Nº 36**

> Every day thousands of people bury good ideas because they are afraid to act on them. And afterwards, the ghosts of these ideas come back to haunt them.
>
> —**DAVID J. SCHWARTZ**
> **Author of *The Magic of Thinking Big***

_____ / _____ / _____

TITLE: _____
(GIVE IT A NAME)

TAG: _____
(DEFINE IT)

STEP ONE
(MAKE THIS SOMETHING YOU CAN DO RIGHT NOW)

_____ ☐

ADDITIONAL STEPS
(THE PLAN)

_____ ☐
_____ ☐
_____ ☐
_____ ☐
_____ ☐

WHY?:
(GIVE IT A PURPOSE)

_____
_____

GENIUS RATING

1   2   3

NOTES   **IDEA Nº 37**

> " My ideas aren't afraid of height. "
>
> —LEENA AHMAD ALMASHAT
> Author of *Harmony Letters*

___ / ___ / _____

TITLE: _____
(GIVE IT A NAME)

TAG: _____
(DEFINE IT)

STEP ONE
(MAKE THIS SOMETHING YOU CAN DO RIGHT NOW)

_____ ☐

ADDITIONAL STEPS
(THE PLAN)

_____ ☐
_____ ☐
_____ ☐
_____ ☐
_____ ☐

WHY?:
(GIVE IT A PURPOSE)

_____
_____

GENIUS RATING

1   **2**   **3**

NOTES **IDEA N⁰ 38**

> " The biggest risk is not taking any risk. In a world that's changing really quickly, the only strategy that is guaranteed to fail is not taking risks. "
>
> —**MARK ZUCKERBERG**
> **Co-founder and CEO of Facebook**

___/___/___

TITLE: _____
(GIVE IT A NAME)

TAG: _____
(DEFINE IT)

STEP ONE
(MAKE THIS SOMETHING YOU CAN DO RIGHT NOW)

_____ ☐

ADDITIONAL STEPS
(THE PLAN)

_____ ☐
_____ ☐
_____ ☐
_____ ☐
_____ ☐

WHY?:
(GIVE IT A PURPOSE)

_____
_____

GENIUS RATING

1   2   3

NOTES **IDEA Nº 39**

> " I have not failed 10,000 times. I have successfully found 10,000 ways that will not work. "
>
> —**THOMAS EDISON**
> **Inventor of the phonograph**

___/___/___

TITLE: _____
(GIVE IT A NAME)

TAG: _____
(DEFINE IT)

STEP ONE
(MAKE THIS SOMETHING YOU CAN DO RIGHT NOW)

_____ ☐

ADDITIONAL STEPS
(THE PLAN)

_____ ☐
_____ ☐
_____ ☐
_____ ☐
_____ ☐

WHY?:
(GIVE IT A PURPOSE)

_____
_____

GENIUS RATING

1   **2**   **3**

NOTES **IDEA N° 40**

> "Timing, perseverance, and ten years of trying will eventually make you look like an overnight success."
>
> **—BIZ STONE**
> **Co-founder of Twitter**

____/____/____

TITLE: _____
(GIVE IT A NAME)

TAG: _____
(DEFINE IT)

STEP ONE
(MAKE THIS SOMETHING YOU CAN DO RIGHT NOW)

_____ ☐

ADDITIONAL STEPS
(THE PLAN)

_____ ☐
_____ ☐
_____ ☐
_____ ☐
_____ ☐

WHY?:
(GIVE IT A PURPOSE)

_____
_____

GENIUS RATING

1 **2** **3**

NOTES   **IDEA Nº 41**

> I get a lot of big ideas, and occasionally I actually come up with one myself.
>
> —**BAUVARD**
> Author of *Some Inspiration for the Overenthusiastic*

___/___/_____

TITLE: _____
(GIVE IT A NAME)

TAG: _____
(DEFINE IT)

STEP ONE
(MAKE THIS SOMETHING YOU CAN DO RIGHT NOW)

_____ ☐

ADDITIONAL STEPS
(THE PLAN)

_____ ☐
_____ ☐
_____ ☐
_____ ☐
_____ ☐

WHY?:
(GIVE IT A PURPOSE)

_____
_____

GENIUS RATING

1   2   3

NOTES   **IDEA N⁰ 42**

> Ideas can come from anywhere and at any time. The problem with making mental notes is that the ink fades very rapidly.
>
> —ROLF SMITH
> **Author of *The 7 Levels of Change***
> **"Colonel Innovation"**

___/___/___

TITLE: _____
(GIVE IT A NAME)

TAG: _____
(DEFINE IT)

STEP ONE
(MAKE THIS SOMETHING YOU CAN DO RIGHT NOW)

_____ ☐

ADDITIONAL STEPS
(THE PLAN)

_____ ☐
_____ ☐
_____ ☐
_____ ☐
_____ ☐

WHY?:
(GIVE IT A PURPOSE)

_____
_____

GENIUS RATING

1 2 3

NOTES **IDEA Nº 43**

> "Where all think alike, no one thinks very much."
>
> —**WALTER LIPPMANN**
> Author of *Public Opinion*

___ / ___ / _____

TITLE: _____
(GIVE IT A NAME)

TAG: _____
(DEFINE IT)

STEP ONE
(MAKE THIS SOMETHING YOU CAN DO RIGHT NOW)

_____ ☐

ADDITIONAL STEPS
(THE PLAN)

_____ ☐
_____ ☐
_____ ☐
_____ ☐
_____ ☐

WHY?:
(GIVE IT A PURPOSE)

_____
_____

GENIUS RATING

1   2   3

NOTES

IDEA N⁰ 44

> Discovery consists of looking at the same thing as everyone else and thinking something different.
>
> —**ALBERT VON SZENT-GYORGY**
> **Biochemist**
> **Nobel Prize in Physiology or Medicine**
> **"Discovered vitamin C"**

___ / ___ / ___

TITLE: _____
(GIVE IT A NAME)

TAG: _____
(DEFINE IT)

STEP ONE
(MAKE THIS SOMETHING YOU CAN DO RIGHT NOW)

_____ ☐

ADDITIONAL STEPS
(THE PLAN)

_____ ☐
_____ ☐
_____ ☐
_____ ☐
_____ ☐

WHY?:
(GIVE IT A PURPOSE)

_____
_____

GENIUS RATING

1   **2**   **3**

NOTES   **IDEA N⁰ 45**

> "Jamming on ideas, rapping on what's next is what entrepreneurs do."
>
> **—TRAVIS KALANICK**
> **Co-founder of Uber**

_____ / ___ / _____

TITLE: _____
(GIVE IT A NAME)

TAG: _____
(DEFINE IT)

STEP ONE

(MAKE THIS SOMETHING YOU CAN DO RIGHT NOW)

☐

ADDITIONAL STEPS

(THE PLAN)

☐
☐
☐
☐
☐

WHY?:
(GIVE IT A PURPOSE)

GENIUS RATING

1 **2** **3**

NOTES **IDEA Nº 46**

> "You don't need to have a 100-person company to develop that idea."
>
> —**LARRY PAGE**
> **Co-founder of Google**

___/___/___

TITLE: _____
(GIVE IT A NAME)

TAG: _____
(DEFINE IT)

STEP ONE
(MAKE THIS SOMETHING YOU CAN DO RIGHT NOW)

_____ ☐

ADDITIONAL STEPS
(THE PLAN)

_____ ☐
_____ ☐
_____ ☐
_____ ☐
_____ ☐

WHY?:
(GIVE IT A PURPOSE)

_____
_____

GENIUS RATING

1   2   3

NOTES   **IDEA N° 47**

> Success doesn't come from what you do occasionally. It comes from what you do consistently.
>
> —MARIE FORLEO
> **Life Coach**
> **Host of *MarieTV***

___ / ___ / ___

TITLE: _____
(GIVE IT A NAME)

TAG: _____
(DEFINE IT)

STEP ONE
(MAKE THIS SOMETHING YOU CAN DO RIGHT NOW)

_____ ☐

ADDITIONAL STEPS
(THE PLAN)

_____ ☐
_____ ☐
_____ ☐
_____ ☐
_____ ☐

WHY?:
(GIVE IT A PURPOSE)

_____
_____

GENIUS RATING

1   2   3

NOTES **IDEA Nº 48**

> "Never say no to an idea. You never know how that idea will ignite another idea."
>
> —STANLEY KUBRICK
> Director of *The Shining*

___ / ___ / ___

TITLE: _____
(GIVE IT A NAME)

TAG: _____
(DEFINE IT)

STEP ONE
(MAKE THIS SOMETHING YOU CAN DO RIGHT NOW)

_____ ☐

ADDITIONAL STEPS
(THE PLAN)

_____ ☐
_____ ☐
_____ ☐
_____ ☐
_____ ☐

WHY?:
(GIVE IT A PURPOSE)

_____
_____

GENIUS RATING

1   2   3

NOTES   **IDEA N⁰ 49**

> "The air is full of ideas. They are knocking you in the head all the time. You only have to know what you want, then forget it and go about your business. Suddenly, the idea will come through. It was there all the time."
>
> —**HENRY FORD**
> **Founder of the Ford Motor Company**

_____ / _____ / _____

TITLE: _____
(GIVE IT A NAME)

TAG: _____
(DEFINE IT)

STEP ONE
(MAKE THIS SOMETHING YOU CAN DO RIGHT NOW)

_____ ☐

ADDITIONAL STEPS
(THE PLAN)

_____ ☐
_____ ☐
_____ ☐
_____ ☐
_____ ☐

WHY?:
(GIVE IT A PURPOSE)

_____
_____

GENIUS RATING

1   **2**   **3**

NOTES **IDEA Nº 50**

> "If you can't fly, run; if you can't run, walk; if you can't walk, crawl; but by all means keep moving."
>
> —**MARTIN LUTHER KING, JR.**
> **Leader in the Civil Rights Movement**

___/___/___

TITLE: _____
(GIVE IT A NAME)

TAG: _____
(DEFINE IT)

STEP ONE
(MAKE THIS SOMETHING YOU CAN DO RIGHT NOW)

_____ ☐

ADDITIONAL STEPS
(THE PLAN)

_____ ☐
_____ ☐
_____ ☐
_____ ☐
_____ ☐

WHY?:
(GIVE IT A PURPOSE)

_____
_____

GENIUS RATING

1   2   3

NOTES   **IDEA Nº 51**

> I'm convinced that about half of what separates the successful entrepreneurs from the non-successful ones is pure perseverance.

—**STEVE JOBS**
Co-founder and CEO of Apple

___ / ___ / ___

TITLE: _____
(GIVE IT A NAME)

TAG: _____
(DEFINE IT)

STEP ONE
(MAKE THIS SOMETHING YOU CAN DO RIGHT NOW)

_____ ☐

ADDITIONAL STEPS
(THE PLAN)

_____ ☐
_____ ☐
_____ ☐
_____ ☐
_____ ☐

WHY?:
(GIVE IT A PURPOSE)

_____
_____

GENIUS RATING

1   2   3

NOTES **IDEA Nº 52**

> *Someday* is a disease that will take your dreams to the grave with you.
>
> —TIM FERRISS
> **Author of *The 4-Hour Work Week***

___/___/___

TITLE: _____
(GIVE IT A NAME)

TAG: _____
(DEFINE IT)

STEP ONE
(MAKE THIS SOMETHING YOU CAN DO RIGHT NOW)

_____ ☐

ADDITIONAL STEPS
(THE PLAN)

_____ ☐
_____ ☐
_____ ☐
_____ ☐
_____ ☐

WHY?:
(GIVE IT A PURPOSE)

_____
_____

GENIUS RATING

1   2   3

NOTES   **IDEA N° 53**

> What is not started today is never finished tomorrow.
>
> —JOHANN WOLFGANG VON GOETHE
> Author, Poet, and Playwright
> *The Sorcerer's Apprentice*

_____ / ___ / _____

TITLE: _____
(GIVE IT A NAME)

TAG: _____
(DEFINE IT)
_____

STEP ONE
(MAKE THIS SOMETHING YOU CAN DO RIGHT NOW)

_____ ☐

ADDITIONAL STEPS
(THE PLAN)

_____ ☐
_____ ☐
_____ ☐
_____ ☐
_____ ☐

WHY?:
(GIVE IT A PURPOSE)

_____
_____

GENIUS RATING

1   2   3

NOTES **IDEA N° 54**

> "I have lots of ideas. How do I pick the right one? Execute on as many as possible. The right idea will pick you."
>
> —**JAMES ALTUCHER**
> **Author of *The Choose Yourself Guide To Wealth***

_____ / _____ / _____

TITLE: _____
(GIVE IT A NAME)

TAG: _____
(DEFINE IT)

STEP ONE
(MAKE THIS SOMETHING YOU CAN DO RIGHT NOW)

_____ ☐

ADDITIONAL STEPS
(THE PLAN)

_____ ☐
_____ ☐
_____ ☐
_____ ☐
_____ ☐

WHY?:
(GIVE IT A PURPOSE)

_____
_____

GENIUS RATING

1   **2**   **3**

NOTES   **IDEA N° 55**

> Success isn't about how much money you make, it's about the difference you make in people's lives.

—**MICHELLE OBAMA**
Former First Lady of the United States

____/____/____

TITLE: _____
(GIVE IT A NAME)

TAG: _____
(DEFINE IT)

STEP ONE
(MAKE THIS SOMETHING YOU CAN DO RIGHT NOW)

_____ ☐

ADDITIONAL STEPS
(THE PLAN)

_____ ☐
_____ ☐
_____ ☐
_____ ☐
_____ ☐

WHY?:
(GIVE IT A PURPOSE)

_____
_____

GENIUS RATING

1   **2**   **3**

NOTES   **IDEA Nº 56**

> Effort is grossly underrated.

—**GARY VAYNERCHUK**
Co-founder and CEO of VaynerMedia

___/___/___

TITLE: _____
(GIVE IT A NAME)

TAG: _____
(DEFINE IT)

STEP ONE
(MAKE THIS SOMETHING YOU CAN DO RIGHT NOW)

_____ ☐

ADDITIONAL STEPS
(THE PLAN)

_____ ☐
_____ ☐
_____ ☐
_____ ☐
_____ ☐

WHY?:
(GIVE IT A PURPOSE)

_____
_____

GENIUS RATING

1   2   3

NOTES   **IDEA N° 57**

> If you want to build something great, you should focus on what the change is that you want to make in the world.
>
> **—MARK ZUCKERBERG**
> **Co-founder and CEO of Facebook**

_____/_____/_____

TITLE: _____
(GIVE IT A NAME)

TAG: _____
(DEFINE IT)

STEP ONE
(MAKE THIS SOMETHING YOU CAN DO RIGHT NOW)

_____ ☐

ADDITIONAL STEPS
(THE PLAN)

_____ ☐
_____ ☐
_____ ☐
_____ ☐
_____ ☐

WHY?:
(GIVE IT A PURPOSE)

_____
_____

GENIUS RATING

1　　**2**　　**3**

NOTES

IDEA N⁰ 58

> Sometimes it is the people no one can imagine anything of who do the things no one can imagine.

—ALAN TURING
Computer Scientist
"The father of artificial intelligence"

___ / ___ / _____

TITLE: _____
(GIVE IT A NAME)

TAG: _____
(DEFINE IT)

STEP ONE
(MAKE THIS SOMETHING YOU CAN DO RIGHT NOW)

☐
_____

ADDITIONAL STEPS
(THE PLAN)

☐
☐
☐
☐
☐
_____
_____
_____
_____
_____

WHY?:
(GIVE IT A PURPOSE)

_____
_____

GENIUS RATING

1   2   3

NOTES   **IDEA N° 59**

> It always seems impossible until it's done.
>
> —**NELSON MANDELA**
> **Former President of South Africa**
> **Author of *The Long Walk to Freedom***

___ / ___ / _____

TITLE: _____
(GIVE IT A NAME)

TAG: _____
(DEFINE IT)

STEP ONE
(MAKE THIS SOMETHING YOU CAN DO RIGHT NOW)

_____ ☐

ADDITIONAL STEPS
(THE PLAN)

_____ ☐
_____ ☐
_____ ☐
_____ ☐
_____ ☐

WHY?:
(GIVE IT A PURPOSE)

_____
_____

GENIUS RATING

1   2   3

NOTES   **IDEA Nº 60**

> If I have a thousand ideas and only one turns out to be good, I am satisfied.

—**ALFRED NOBLE**
Inventor of dynamite
Benefactor of the Nobel Prize

___ / ___ / ___

TITLE: _____
(GIVE IT A NAME)

TAG: _____
(DEFINE IT)

STEP ONE
(MAKE THIS SOMETHING YOU CAN DO RIGHT NOW)

_____ ☐

ADDITIONAL STEPS
(THE PLAN)

_____ ☐
_____ ☐
_____ ☐
_____ ☐
_____ ☐

WHY?:
(GIVE IT A PURPOSE)

_____
_____

GENIUS RATING

1   2   3

NOTES **IDEA Nº 61**

> Whether you think you can or think you can't, you're right.

—**HENRY FORD**
Founder of the Ford Motor Company

___ / ___ / _____

TITLE: _____
(GIVE IT A NAME)

TAG: _____
(DEFINE IT)

STEP ONE
(MAKE THIS SOMETHING YOU CAN DO RIGHT NOW)

_____ ☐

ADDITIONAL STEPS
(THE PLAN)

_____ ☐
_____ ☐
_____ ☐
_____ ☐
_____ ☐

WHY?:
(GIVE IT A PURPOSE)

_____
_____

GENIUS RATING

1   **2**   **3**

NOTES **IDEA N° 62**

> Everyone who's ever taken a shower has had an idea. It's the person who gets out of the shower, dries off and does something about it who makes a difference.

—**NOLAN BUSHNELL**
Co-founder of Atari

___/___/___

TITLE: _____
(GIVE IT A NAME)

TAG: _____
(DEFINE IT)

STEP ONE
(MAKE THIS SOMETHING YOU CAN DO RIGHT NOW)

☐
_____

ADDITIONAL STEPS
(THE PLAN)

_____ ☐
_____ ☐
_____ ☐
_____ ☐
_____ ☐

WHY?:
(GIVE IT A PURPOSE)

_____
_____

GENIUS RATING

1   **2**   **3**

NOTES **IDEA Nº 63**

> One thing I learnt was never to hoard ideas because either they are not so relevant or they've gone stale. Whatever it is, pour them out.

—**MARY QUANT**
Fashion Designer
"Popularised the Mini Skirt"

_____ / _____ / _____

TITLE: _____
(GIVE IT A NAME)

TAG: _____
(DEFINE IT)

STEP ONE
(MAKE THIS SOMETHING YOU CAN DO RIGHT NOW)

_____ ☐

ADDITIONAL STEPS
(THE PLAN)

_____ ☐
_____ ☐
_____ ☐
_____ ☐
_____ ☐

WHY?:
(GIVE IT A PURPOSE)

_____
_____

GENIUS RATING

1 **2** **3**

NOTES **IDEA N° 64**

> Get a good idea and stay with it. Dog it, and work at it until it's done right.

—WALT DISNEY
Co-founder of The Walt Disney Company

_____ / _____ / _____

TITLE: _____
(GIVE IT A NAME)

TAG: _____
(DEFINE IT)

STEP ONE
(MAKE THIS SOMETHING YOU CAN DO RIGHT NOW)

_____ ☐

ADDITIONAL STEPS
(THE PLAN)

_____ ☐
_____ ☐
_____ ☐
_____ ☐
_____ ☐

WHY?:
(GIVE IT A PURPOSE)

_____
_____

GENIUS RATING

1   2   3

NOTES **IDEA N° 65**

> " It is the essence of genius to make use of the simplest ideas. "
>
> —CHARLES PÉGUY
> Poet, *Le Mystère de la Charité de Jeanne d'Arc*

___/___/___

TITLE: _____
(GIVE IT A NAME)

TAG: _____
(DEFINE IT)
_____

STEP ONE
(MAKE THIS SOMETHING YOU CAN DO RIGHT NOW)

_____ ☐

ADDITIONAL STEPS
(THE PLAN)

_____ ☐
_____ ☐
_____ ☐
_____ ☐
_____ ☐

WHY?:
(GIVE IT A PURPOSE)

_____
_____

GENIUS RATING

1   2   3

NOTES   **IDEA N⁰ 66**

> Ideas won't keep. Something must be done about them.
>
> —**ALFRED NORTH WHITEHEAD**
> **Mathematician and Philosopher**
> **Author of *Process and Reality***

___/___/___

TITLE: _____
(GIVE IT A NAME)

TAG: _____
(DEFINE IT)

STEP ONE
(MAKE THIS SOMETHING YOU CAN DO RIGHT NOW)

_____ ☐

ADDITIONAL STEPS
(THE PLAN)

_____ ☐
_____ ☐
_____ ☐
_____ ☐
_____ ☐

WHY?:
(GIVE IT A PURPOSE)

_____
_____

GENIUS RATING

1   **2**   **3**

NOTES   **IDEA N° 67**

> Dream big. Start small. But most of all, start.
>
> —SIMON SINEK
> Author of *Start With Why*

_____ / ____ / _____

TITLE: _____
(GIVE IT A NAME)

TAG: _____
(DEFINE IT)

STEP ONE

(MAKE THIS SOMETHING YOU CAN DO RIGHT NOW)

☐

ADDITIONAL STEPS

(THE PLAN)

☐
☐
☐
☐
☐

WHY?:
(GIVE IT A PURPOSE)

GENIUS RATING

1   **2**   **3**

NOTES **IDEA N⁰ 68**

> " A year from now you may wish you had started today. "
>
> —KAREN LAMB
> Author of *Thea Astley: Inventing Her Own Weather*

___ / ___ / ___

TITLE: _____
(GIVE IT A NAME)

TAG: _____
(DEFINE IT)

STEP ONE
(MAKE THIS SOMETHING YOU CAN DO RIGHT NOW)

_____ ☐

ADDITIONAL STEPS
(THE PLAN)

_____ ☐
_____ ☐
_____ ☐
_____ ☐
_____ ☐

WHY?:
(GIVE IT A PURPOSE)

_____
_____

GENIUS RATING

1   **2**   **3**

NOTES   **IDEA N° 69**

> It seems to be one of the paradoxes of creativity that in order to think originally, we must familiarise ourselves with the ideas of others.
>
> —**GEORGE F. KNELLER**
> **Author of *The Art and Science of Creativity***

___ / ___ / ___

TITLE: _____
(GIVE IT A NAME)

TAG: _____
(DEFINE IT)

STEP ONE
(MAKE THIS SOMETHING YOU CAN DO RIGHT NOW)

_____ ☐

ADDITIONAL STEPS
(THE PLAN)

_____ ☐
_____ ☐
_____ ☐
_____ ☐
_____ ☐

WHY?:
(GIVE IT A PURPOSE)

_____
_____

GENIUS RATING

1   **2**   **3**

NOTES   **IDEA Nº 70**

> "The question isn't who is going to let me; it's who is going to stop me?"
>
> **—AYN RAND**
> **Author of *The Fountainhead***

___ / ___ / _____

TITLE: _____
(GIVE IT A NAME)

TAG: _____
(DEFINE IT)

STEP ONE
(MAKE THIS SOMETHING YOU CAN DO RIGHT NOW)

_____ ☐

ADDITIONAL STEPS
(THE PLAN)

_____ ☐
_____ ☐
_____ ☐
_____ ☐
_____ ☐

WHY?:
(GIVE IT A PURPOSE)

_____
_____

GENIUS RATING

1   **2**   **3**

NOTES **IDEA Nº 71**

> Don't be indifferent about any random idea that occurs to you, because each and every idea is for a particular purpose. It may not be beneficial to you, but can be what others are craving for.
>
> **—MICHAEL BASSEY JOHNSON**
> **Author of *The Creative Power***

___/___/___

TITLE: _____
(GIVE IT A NAME)

TAG: _____
(DEFINE IT)

STEP ONE
(MAKE THIS SOMETHING YOU CAN DO RIGHT NOW)

_____ ☐

ADDITIONAL STEPS
(THE PLAN)

_____ ☐
_____ ☐
_____ ☐
_____ ☐
_____ ☐

WHY?:
(GIVE IT A PURPOSE)

_____
_____

GENIUS RATING

1   2   3

NOTES   **IDEA Nº 72**

> "Nothing like a night-time stroll to give you ideas."
>
> —J. K. ROWLING
> **Author of the *Harry Potter* series**

_____ / ____ / _____

TITLE: _____
(GIVE IT A NAME)

TAG: _____
(DEFINE IT)

STEP ONE
(MAKE THIS SOMETHING YOU CAN DO RIGHT NOW)

☐

ADDITIONAL STEPS
(THE PLAN)

☐
☐
☐
☐
☐

WHY?:
(GIVE IT A PURPOSE)

GENIUS RATING

1   2   3

NOTES **IDEA Nº 73**

> "Focus on being productive instead of busy."

—TIM FERRISS
Author of *The 4-Hour Work Week*

___ / ___ / _____

TITLE: _____
(GIVE IT A NAME)

TAG: _____
(DEFINE IT)

STEP ONE
(MAKE THIS SOMETHING YOU CAN DO RIGHT NOW)

_____ ☐

ADDITIONAL STEPS
(THE PLAN)

_____ ☐
_____ ☐
_____ ☐
_____ ☐
_____ ☐

WHY?:
(GIVE IT A PURPOSE)

_____
_____

GENIUS RATING

1   **2**   **3**

NOTES **IDEA N⁰ 74**

> First comes thought, then organization of that thought into ideas and plans, then transformation of those plans into reality. The beginning, as you will observe, is in your imagination.

—**NAPOLEON HILL**
Author of *Think and Grow Rich*

___ / ___ / _____

TITLE: _____
(GIVE IT A NAME)

TAG: _____
(DEFINE IT)

STEP ONE
(MAKE THIS SOMETHING YOU CAN DO RIGHT NOW)

_____ ☐

ADDITIONAL STEPS
(THE PLAN)

_____ ☐
_____ ☐
_____ ☐
_____ ☐
_____ ☐

WHY?:
(GIVE IT A PURPOSE)

_____
_____

GENIUS RATING

1   2   3

NOTES   **IDEA Nº 75**

> It's not about ideas. It's about making ideas happen.
>
> —SCOTT BELSKY
> **Co-founder of Behance**

___ / ___ / ___

TITLE: _____
(GIVE IT A NAME)

TAG: _____
(DEFINE IT)

STEP ONE
(MAKE THIS SOMETHING YOU CAN DO RIGHT NOW)

_____ ☐

ADDITIONAL STEPS
(THE PLAN)

_____ ☐
_____ ☐
_____ ☐
_____ ☐
_____ ☐

WHY?:
(GIVE IT A PURPOSE)

_____
_____

GENIUS RATING

1   2   3

NOTES   **IDEA Nº 76**

> "Someone is sitting in the shade today because someone planted a tree a long time ago."
>
> —**WARREN BUFFETT**
> **Investor**
> **CEO of Berkshire Hathaway**

___ / ___ / _____

TITLE: _____
(GIVE IT A NAME)

TAG: _____
(DEFINE IT)

STEP ONE
(MAKE THIS SOMETHING YOU CAN DO RIGHT NOW)

_____ ☐

ADDITIONAL STEPS
(THE PLAN)

_____ ☐
_____ ☐
_____ ☐
_____ ☐
_____ ☐

WHY?:
(GIVE IT A PURPOSE)

_____
_____

GENIUS RATING

1   **2**   **3**

NOTES **IDEA N° 77**

> "Building a business is not rocket science, it's about having a great idea and seeing it through with integrity."
>
> —**RICHARD BRANSON**
> **Founder of the Virgin Group**

___/___/___

TITLE: _____
(GIVE IT A NAME)

TAG: _____
(DEFINE IT)

STEP ONE
(MAKE THIS SOMETHING YOU CAN DO RIGHT NOW)

_____ ☐

ADDITIONAL STEPS
(THE PLAN)

_____ ☐
_____ ☐
_____ ☐
_____ ☐
_____ ☐

WHY?:
(GIVE IT A PURPOSE)

_____
_____

GENIUS RATING

1   2   3

NOTES   **IDEA Nº 78**

> Nearly everyone who develops an idea works it up to the point where it looks impossible and then gets discouraged. That's not the place to become discouraged.

—**THOMAS EDISON**
Inventor of the phonograph

___/___/___

TITLE: _____
(GIVE IT A NAME)

TAG: _____
(DEFINE IT)

STEP ONE
(MAKE THIS SOMETHING YOU CAN DO RIGHT NOW)

_____ ☐

ADDITIONAL STEPS
(THE PLAN)

_____ ☐
_____ ☐
_____ ☐
_____ ☐
_____ ☐

WHY?:
(GIVE IT A PURPOSE)

_____
_____

GENIUS RATING

1   2   3

NOTES **IDEA N⁰ 79**

> "The secret to getting ahead is getting started."
>
> —**MARK TWAIN**
> **Author of *Adventures of Huckleberry Finn***

_____ / _____ / _____

TITLE: _____
(GIVE IT A NAME)

TAG: _____
(DEFINE IT)

STEP ONE
(MAKE THIS SOMETHING YOU CAN DO RIGHT NOW)

_____ ☐

ADDITIONAL STEPS
(THE PLAN)

_____ ☐
_____ ☐
_____ ☐
_____ ☐
_____ ☐

WHY?:
(GIVE IT A PURPOSE)

_____
_____

GENIUS RATING

1   2   3

NOTES **IDEA N° 80**

> " Other people see things and say *why*? But I dream things that never were and I say *why not*? "
>
> —JOHN F. KENNEDY
> 35th U.S. President

___ / ___ / _____

TITLE: _____
(GIVE IT A NAME)

TAG: _____
(DEFINE IT)

STEP ONE
(MAKE THIS SOMETHING YOU CAN DO RIGHT NOW)

_____ ☐

ADDITIONAL STEPS
(THE PLAN)

_____ ☐
_____ ☐
_____ ☐
_____ ☐
_____ ☐

WHY?:
(GIVE IT A PURPOSE)

_____
_____

GENIUS RATING

1   2   3

NOTES **IDEA N° 81**

> "All great deeds and all great thoughts have a ridiculous beginning."
>
> —ALBERT CAMUS
> Philosopher
> Author of *The Rebel*

___ / ___ / ___

TITLE: _____
(GIVE IT A NAME)

TAG: _____
(DEFINE IT)

STEP ONE
(MAKE THIS SOMETHING YOU CAN DO RIGHT NOW)

_____ ☐

ADDITIONAL STEPS
(THE PLAN)

_____ ☐
_____ ☐
_____ ☐
_____ ☐
_____ ☐

WHY?:
(GIVE IT A PURPOSE)

_____
_____

GENIUS RATING

1   2   3

NOTES **IDEA N° 82**

> Don't worry about people stealing your ideas. If your ideas are any good, you'll have to ram them down people's throats.

—**HOWARD AIKEN**
Physicist
Designer of the Mark 1 electromagnetic computer

___ / ___ / ___

TITLE: _____
(GIVE IT A NAME)

TAG: _____
(DEFINE IT)

STEP ONE

(MAKE THIS SOMETHING YOU CAN DO RIGHT NOW)

_____ ☐

ADDITIONAL STEPS

(THE PLAN)

_____ ☐
_____ ☐
_____ ☐
_____ ☐
_____ ☐

WHY?:
(GIVE IT A PURPOSE)

_____
_____

GENIUS RATING

1   **2**   **3**

NOTES **IDEA Nº 83**

> " Imagination is more important than knowledge. "
>
> —ALBERT EINSTEIN
> **Theoretical Physicist, The Theory of Relativity**

____/____/____

TITLE: _____
(GIVE IT A NAME)

TAG: _____
(DEFINE IT)

STEP ONE
(MAKE THIS SOMETHING YOU CAN DO RIGHT NOW)

_____ ☐

ADDITIONAL STEPS
(THE PLAN)

_____ ☐
_____ ☐
_____ ☐
_____ ☐
_____ ☐

WHY?:
(GIVE IT A PURPOSE)

_____
_____

GENIUS RATING

1   **2**   **3**

NOTES **IDEA Nº 84**

> " Don't waste a single second. Just move forward as fast as you can, and go for it. "

—**REBECCA WOODCOCK**
Founder of CakeHealth

___/___/___

TITLE: _____
(GIVE IT A NAME)

TAG: _____
(DEFINE IT)

STEP ONE
(MAKE THIS SOMETHING YOU CAN DO RIGHT NOW)

_____ ☐

ADDITIONAL STEPS
(THE PLAN)

_____ ☐
_____ ☐
_____ ☐
_____ ☐
_____ ☐

WHY?:
(GIVE IT A PURPOSE)

_____
_____

GENIUS RATING

1   2   3

NOTES   **IDEA Nº 85**

> Sometimes it's important to wake up and stop dreaming. When a really great dream shows up, grab it.
>
> **—LARRY PAGE**
> **Co-founder of Google**

___/___/___

TITLE: _____
(GIVE IT A NAME)

TAG: _____
(DEFINE IT)

STEP ONE
(MAKE THIS SOMETHING YOU CAN DO RIGHT NOW)

_____ ☐

ADDITIONAL STEPS
(THE PLAN)

_____ ☐
_____ ☐
_____ ☐
_____ ☐
_____ ☐

WHY?:
(GIVE IT A PURPOSE)

_____
_____

GENIUS RATING

1   2   3

NOTES **IDEA Nº 86**

“ I begin with an idea and then it becomes something else. ”

—PABLO PICASSO
Painter
Pioneer of the Cubist movement

___/___/___

TITLE: _____
(GIVE IT A NAME)

TAG: _____
(DEFINE IT)

STEP ONE
(MAKE THIS SOMETHING YOU CAN DO RIGHT NOW)

_____ ☐

ADDITIONAL STEPS
(THE PLAN)

_____ ☐
_____ ☐
_____ ☐
_____ ☐
_____ ☐

WHY?:
(GIVE IT A PURPOSE)

_____
_____

GENIUS RATING

1   **2**   **3**

NOTES   **IDEA N° 87**

> Innovation is taking two things that already exist and putting them together in a new way.

—**TOM FRESTON**
Co-founder of MTV

___ / ___ / _____

TITLE: _____
(GIVE IT A NAME)

TAG: _____
_____
(DEFINE IT)

STEP ONE
(MAKE THIS SOMETHING YOU CAN DO RIGHT NOW)

_____ ☐

ADDITIONAL STEPS
(THE PLAN)

_____ ☐
_____ ☐
_____ ☐
_____ ☐
_____ ☐

WHY?:
(GIVE IT A PURPOSE)

_____
_____

GENIUS RATING

1   2   3

NOTES   **IDEA N⁰ 88**

> There's a way to do it better. Find it.

—THOMAS EDISON
Inventor of the phonograph

____ / ____ / _____

TITLE: _____
(GIVE IT A NAME)

TAG: _____
(DEFINE IT)

STEP ONE
(MAKE THIS SOMETHING YOU CAN DO RIGHT NOW)

_____ ☐

ADDITIONAL STEPS
(THE PLAN)

_____ ☐
_____ ☐
_____ ☐
_____ ☐
_____ ☐

WHY?:
(GIVE IT A PURPOSE)

_____
_____

GENIUS RATING

1   2   3

NOTES **IDEA N° 89**

> It's easy to come up with new ideas; the hard part is letting go of what worked for you two years ago, but will soon be out of date.
>
> —ROGER VON OECH
> **Inventor and Toy Maker**
> **Author of *A Whack on the Side of the Head***

_____ / ___ / _____

TITLE: _____
(GIVE IT A NAME)

TAG: _____
(DEFINE IT)

STEP ONE
(MAKE THIS SOMETHING YOU CAN DO RIGHT NOW)

_____ ☐

ADDITIONAL STEPS
(THE PLAN)

_____ ☐
_____ ☐
_____ ☐
_____ ☐
_____ ☐

WHY?:
(GIVE IT A PURPOSE)

_____
_____

GENIUS RATING

1   2   3

NOTES **IDEA N⁰ 90**

> When everything seems to be going against you, remember that the airplane takes off against the wind, not with it.

—**HENRY FORD**
Founder of the Ford Motor Company

___/___/___

TITLE: _____
(GIVE IT A NAME)

TAG: _____
(DEFINE IT)

STEP ONE
(MAKE THIS SOMETHING YOU CAN DO RIGHT NOW)

_____ ☐

ADDITIONAL STEPS
(THE PLAN)

_____ ☐
_____ ☐
_____ ☐
_____ ☐
_____ ☐

WHY?:
(GIVE IT A PURPOSE)

_____
_____

GENIUS RATING

1   **2**   **3**

NOTES **IDEA Nº 91**

> "A lot of people don't just go ahead and try things."

—**PIERRE OMIDYAR**
Founder of eBay

_____ / _____ / _____

TITLE: _____
(GIVE IT A NAME)

TAG: _____
(DEFINE IT)

STEP ONE
(MAKE THIS SOMETHING YOU CAN DO RIGHT NOW)

_____ ☐

ADDITIONAL STEPS
(THE PLAN)

_____ ☐
_____ ☐
_____ ☐
_____ ☐
_____ ☐

WHY?:
(GIVE IT A PURPOSE)

_____
_____

GENIUS RATING

1   **2**   **3**

NOTES   **IDEA Nº 92**

> To any entrepreneur: if you want to do it, do it now. If you don't, you're going to regret it.
>
> **—CATHERINE COOK**
> **Co-founder of MyYearbook**

___/___/___

TITLE: _____
(GIVE IT A NAME)

TAG: _____
(DEFINE IT)

STEP ONE
(MAKE THIS SOMETHING YOU CAN DO RIGHT NOW)

_____ ☐

ADDITIONAL STEPS
(THE PLAN)

_____ ☐
_____ ☐
_____ ☐
_____ ☐
_____ ☐

WHY?:
(GIVE IT A PURPOSE)

_____
_____

GENIUS RATING

1   2   3

NOTES   **IDEA N° 93**

> Could *Hamlet* have been written by a committee, or the *Mona Lisa* painted by a club? Could the New Testament have been composed as a conference report? Creative ideas do not spring from groups. They spring from individuals.
>
> —**A. WHITNEY GRISWOLD**
> **16th President of Yale University**

___/___/___

TITLE: _____
(GIVE IT A NAME)

TAG: _____
(DEFINE IT)

STEP ONE
(MAKE THIS SOMETHING YOU CAN DO RIGHT NOW)

_____ ☐

ADDITIONAL STEPS
(THE PLAN)

_____ ☐
_____ ☐
_____ ☐
_____ ☐
_____ ☐

WHY?:
(GIVE IT A PURPOSE)

_____
_____

GENIUS RATING

1   **2**   **3**

NOTES   **IDEA Nº 94**

> All achievements, all earned riches, have their beginning in an idea.
>
> —**NAPOLEON HILL**
> **Author of *Think and Grow Rich***

___/___/___

TITLE: _____
(GIVE IT A NAME)

TAG: _____
(DEFINE IT)

STEP ONE
(MAKE THIS SOMETHING YOU CAN DO RIGHT NOW)

_____ ☐

ADDITIONAL STEPS
(THE PLAN)

_____ ☐
_____ ☐
_____ ☐
_____ ☐
_____ ☐

WHY?:
(GIVE IT A PURPOSE)

_____
_____

GENIUS RATING

1   **2**   **3**

NOTES   **IDEA N° 95**

> The idea is like grass. It craves light, likes crowds, thrives on cross breeding, grows better for being stepped on.

—**URSULA K. LE GUIN**
Author of *The Left Hand of Darkness*
"Grandmaster of Science Fiction"

___/___/___

TITLE: _____
(GIVE IT A NAME)

TAG: _____
(DEFINE IT)

STEP ONE
(MAKE THIS SOMETHING YOU CAN DO RIGHT NOW)

_____ ☐

ADDITIONAL STEPS
(THE PLAN)

_____ ☐
_____ ☐
_____ ☐
_____ ☐
_____ ☐

WHY?:
(GIVE IT A PURPOSE)

_____
_____

GENIUS RATING

1   2   3

NOTES   **IDEA N° 96**

> A good idea is something that does not solve just one single problem, but rather can solve multiple problems at once.
>
> **—SHIGERU MIYAMOTO**
> **Video game designer**
> **Co-representative director of Nintendo**

_____ / _____ / _____

TITLE: _____
(GIVE IT A NAME)

TAG: _____
(DEFINE IT)

STEP ONE
(MAKE THIS SOMETHING YOU CAN DO RIGHT NOW)

_____ ☐

ADDITIONAL STEPS
(THE PLAN)

_____ ☐
_____ ☐
_____ ☐
_____ ☐
_____ ☐

WHY?:
(GIVE IT A PURPOSE)

_____
_____

GENIUS RATING

1   **2**   **3**

NOTES   **IDEA Nº 97**

> If coming up with ten ideas sounds too hard, then come up with twenty.
>
> —JAMES ALTUCHER
> Author of *The Choose Yourself Guide to Wealth*

___ / ___ / ___

TITLE: _____
(GIVE IT A NAME)

TAG: _____
(DEFINE IT)

STEP ONE
(MAKE THIS SOMETHING YOU CAN DO RIGHT NOW)

_____ ☐

ADDITIONAL STEPS
(THE PLAN)

_____ ☐
_____ ☐
_____ ☐
_____ ☐
_____ ☐

WHY?:
(GIVE IT A PURPOSE)

_____
_____

GENIUS RATING

1   2   3

NOTES **IDEA N° 98**

> "What do you need to start a business? Three simple things: know your product better than anyone, know your customer, and have a burning desire to succeed."
>
> —DAVE THOMAS
> **Founder of Wendy's**

____/____/____

TITLE: _____
(GIVE IT A NAME)

TAG: _____
(DEFINE IT)

STEP ONE
(MAKE THIS SOMETHING YOU CAN DO RIGHT NOW)

_____ ☐

ADDITIONAL STEPS
(THE PLAN)

_____ ☐
_____ ☐
_____ ☐
_____ ☐
_____ ☐

WHY?:
(GIVE IT A PURPOSE)

_____
_____

GENIUS RATING

1   2   3

NOTES   **IDEA Nº 99**

> When you innovate, you've got to be prepared for people telling you that you are nuts.
>
> **—LARRY ELLISON**
> **Co-founder of Oracle Corporation**

_____/_____/_____

TITLE: _____
(GIVE IT A NAME)

TAG: _____
(DEFINE IT)

STEP ONE

(MAKE THIS SOMETHING YOU CAN DO RIGHT NOW)

_____ ☐

ADDITIONAL STEPS

(THE PLAN)

_____ ☐
_____ ☐
_____ ☐
_____ ☐
_____ ☐

WHY?:
(GIVE IT A PURPOSE)

_____
_____

GENIUS RATING

1   2   3

NOTES   **IDEA N⁰ 100**

> If you can dream it, you can do it.
>
> **—WALT DISNEY**
> **Co-founder of the Walt Disney Company**

congratulations

That's one small journal, 100 big ideas.